LinkedIn or LinkedOut?

107 Ways to Grow Your Business using LinkedIn™

By Sam Rathling & Derek Reilly

Copyright by Sam Rathling & Associates 2013 ©

http://samrathling.com

http://derekreilly.com

Table of Contents

Chapter Content	Page No.
Who Was This Book Written For?	3
How to Use This Book	5
15 Tips for Your LinkedIn Personal Profile	9
15 Tips for Growing Your Connections to 500+	19
10 Tips for LinkedIn Status Updates	29
10 Tips for Finding, Approaching & Managing Contacts	37
10 Tips for Your LinkedIn Company Profile	45
10 Tips for LinkedIn Recommendations	51
10 Tips for LinkedIn Groups	57
10 Tips to Become the 'Go-To' Expert in Your Niche	63
10 Tips for Extra LinkedIn Learning	73
7 Additional Tips to help you win more business from LinkedIn	77
Free Chapter from best-selling book 'GIVE'	83
About the Author – Sam Rathling	95
About the Author – Derek Reilly	97
Before you go…	99

Who Was This Book Written For?

This book was written for owners of small businesses who simply have no time or patience when it comes to LinkedIn and other forms of online networking. You are probably too busy to take a full day out of the business to go on a LinkedIn training course, where you know you would learn loads, but implement none of the great tips because you are just too busy being busy.

You want someone to give you an easy to understand, simple and practical guide that will be effective for your business and take very little time to implement. As a small business owner myself, I know and appreciate the pressure you are under and believe me if someone had given me this book at the start of my LinkedIn journey, I would not have had to spend years and years trying to work it out.

You really can get massive business opportunities and new clients from what is simply a phenomenal sales and networking tool (if you know how). You will really like this book and benefit hugely from it if:

- You have no profile at all on LinkedIn and are starting from scratch

- You already have a profile on LinkedIn but can't remember the last time you looked at it

- You are using LinkedIn already but currently do not get any business from it

- You have limited time to spend on LinkedIn although you know it's important to your business

- You are ready to take your online reputation and your business to the next level

- You want to position yourself as the 'go-to' expert in your field

- You know your target market is on LinkedIn but you have no clue how to gain access to them

- You have employees that you could replicate this advice to

- You have less than 10 minutes a day to spend on networking sites like LinkedIn

This book was written for every busy Entrepreneur that knows the huge potential of LinkedIn, but has no idea how to unlock it. There are many resources available on the subject of LinkedIn. You can access thousands of free articles and blogs out there about how to make LinkedIn work for your business, so why choose this one? What we have done here is pull it all together, wrap the information up into 107 easy and simple steps, almost like a checklist that you can work from and dip in and out of as and when you have the time.

If you put aside 1 hour a week for the next 4 weeks you would be able to completely revamp your LinkedIn presence and start to see an increase in visits to your profile, an increase in the number of people attracted to your profile and a significant increase in the amount of times you show up in search results. In 2012, a staggering 5.7 billion searches took place in LinkedIn's search bar. If you are not being found on LinkedIn, then you can be assured that your competitors are. We wrote this book to make sure it's your profile they are looking at and not your competitors!

How to Use This Book

This book should be used as a checklist of tips for you to implement. Depending on your current knowledge of LinkedIn and how much you use it, you may find that some of the items on the list of 105 tips are already in place for your LinkedIn profile. If so just quickly move on to the next one. I know that your time is precious and I would not want to waste it!

We have made things very easy for you by providing a downloadable checklist with all 107 tips listed so that you can simply mark them off as you complete each one.

Visit this link to download this list completely free:

http://samrathling.com/107-Tips-Checklist-For-LinkedIn

The checklist won't mean much to you if you choose not to go on and read the book, especially if you are pretty new to LinkedIn or if you don't use LinkedIn that much today as this list doesn't give any explanations. That's all coming up in the book. Our purpose in writing this is simple. We want to help you win more clients, and the more tips you complete from the list of 107 ways to do this, the better your chances of securing new business opportunities from LinkedIn.

The way this book is written, you would be able to delegate many of the tips to your staff if you have a team around you. We have also written this with your team in mind, if you do employ staff then every single one of them should also implement these tips on their own LinkedIn profile. Why not gift this book to every employee as a thank you for their hard work, and in return your business will massively benefit from the maximum exposure you will get.

Having an increased online presence and a wider network from each of the team will really give you an added edge over your competitors. You never know, you may find a LinkedIn whizz in the team who fancies taking on more responsibility in this area and could really ramp up your LinkedIn presence as a business.

One of the co-Authors of this book, Sam Rathling, wrote about this in the book 'GIVE: 16 Giving Strategies To Grow Your Business'. You will find some great chapters on saying thank you, giving responsibility, staff happiness, employee engagement and time management. As a thank you for purchasing this book, we have included a bonus chapter for you at the end, enjoy your free gift.

So now that you know how to use this book, let's start by looking at how to win more clients by having a really credible LinkedIn profile.

The VCP Process®

The VCP Process is vital for you to understand if you are to be successful at marketing your business through LinkedIn. This process is usually referred to when we talk about referral marketing, when networking on a face to face basis, and the key is in the power of relationships. The system of information, support and referrals that you assemble from your networks, both online and offline, will be based on your relationships with other individuals and businesses. Referral marketing works because these relationships work both ways and both parties benefit in some way.

A marketing plan where referrals are centric to the success of that plan, involves relationships of many different kinds. Relationships don't just spring up fully grown, they must be nurtured and as they grow, the relationships are fed by mutual trust and shared benefits for each party.

The relationship evolves through three phases: Visibility, Credibility and Profitability. We call this evolution the VCP Process®. First your business and you must be visible, if we discuss the VCP Process in relation to LinkedIn, this is all about you having a presence online, having a personal profile and a company profile and being seen to be active online. When it comes to moving an initial connection through to the next stage, which is Credibility, you must always keep in mind that any successful relationship, whether a personal or a business relationship, is unique to every pair of individuals, and it evolves over time. The relationship starts out tentative, fragile, full of unfulfilled possibilities and expectations. It grows stronger with experience and familiarity, and then it matures into trust and commitment.

Credibility online and especially using LinkedIn is all about how you message your business, how you start and build relationships and how you position yourself through your profiles and in the way you approach relationship building and growing your network. The VCP Process describes the process of creation, growth and strengthening of business, professional and personal relationships. The main problem with people's lack of understanding of this vital process is that they forget the step that involves the 'C', credibility is all about growing and nurturing the relationship before moving to a sale or moving into a place where someone will refer you to one of their clients. All too often we see people using LinkedIn as a selling platform, spamming their network with requests to buy products or services from them, or visit their website. The credibility part is vital if you want to grow your business on LinkedIn.

Only when you add Visibility to Credibility can you move to Profitability in a relationship. When you move the relationship to the next level you will be referred, recommended, promoted and will spread great word of mouth about you and your business. When you are networking online the VCP Process® is even more important as you may not get the chance to actually meet the person you are networking with on a face to face basis. Always bear in mind that V+C = P. This simple concept has made a bigger difference in more people's networking efforts than any other single idea you will come across and should be remembered as you read this book

15 Tips for your LinkedIn Personal Profile

LinkedIn = Personal Profile Complete + Keywords

LinkedOut = Profile incomplete with no personal summary or keywords

Tip 1 – Get Your Name Right

Make sure that the name you use on LinkedIn is actually the name people know you for in business, and matches the name they would search for you on LinkedIn. That way there can be no confusion especially if you don't have a unique name. If you prefer to be called Terence by clients but everyone knows you as Terry then choose the first name that you are most likely to be searched by or the name that fits with your current online profile.

In addition make sure that your business card matches your LinkedIn name, so if you meet someone at an event and they go to connect with you on LinkedIn afterwards that you can be found easily. Sounds simple, however an apostrophe in the wrong place or a double-barrelled name can be the difference between you making a connection and someone not bothering because they couldn't find you easily.

Tip 2 – 100% Profile Complete

The initial goal of any LinkedIn Personal profile is 100% completion, any number less than 100% is simply saying 'I couldn't be bothered'. Less than 100% affects your credibility and this also impacts upon your power to attract new connections. Make sure that each and every section of your profile is complete from your education to your work history, your skills, summary and headline. The other reason for this is the accuracy level you will start to see when LinkedIn begins recommending 'People You May Know'.

This 'People You May Know' feature appears in a few places on LinkedIn and is based on the information which you enter into your Personal Profile. If you do not complete your profile then you have less chance of connecting with someone you know well, that could lead you to a new client or a great big piece of business you were not expecting.

Tip 3 – Your Professional Headline

Your LinkedIn Professional Headline when written well can drive massive opportunities your way, whether that be job offers or new clients. The reality is that most people use this part of their LinkedIn profile to demonstrate their current job title or position and their company name.

The professional headline of your LinkedIn profile is the one short description, 110 characters in length that you can see underneath your name on your profile. It is also what others see when you post an update or when you ask someone to connect with you.

Look at your current professional headline on LinkedIn. If it says your job title or position and company name be prepared to transform your LinkedIn visibility. It is important if you want to get hired for a job or develop new business for your company. This one part of your profile will determine how many times you appear in search results.

It will also determine how many people will want to connect with you and is your chance to set you apart from the competition. By changing these 110 characters to include what you offer and what you want to be found for, you will change your visibility, credibility and profitability on LinkedIn.

The Importance of Keywords and the Professional Headline

As with all web based content, your LinkedIn Professional Headline is keyword searchable. Pick one main keyword or phrase that you want to be found for. Have you got one? Now go to LinkedIn and put in a people search with that keyword or key phrase in the top right corner. Did you appear on the first page? If not then the person who is in the top spot is probably getting the clients that you want!

How Should I write my Headline?

Choose your keywords wisely and you could rocket up the search rankings instantly and appear on the first page of LinkedIn searches. We recommend that you include the keyword or keyword phrase you have picked out, at least twice in your Professional Headline. Make sure these same keywords or keyword phrase also appear in other parts of your LinkedIn profile as well, especially in your current job title.

What else can I do to Improve my Professional Headline?

Focusing on the end benefit to the customer is another good way to grab attention. Always remember to include the keyword/search term twice:

Example 1

Old Headline "Nutritionist"

New Headline: "The Nutritionist Who Increases Staff Happiness – Nutritionist who reduces absenteeism in the workplace"

Example 2

Old Headline: "Recruitment Consultant"

New Headline: "Changing the way the world does recruitment, saving you time and money with fixed price, low cost recruitment"

Example 3

Old Headline: "Business Coach"

New Headline: "Business Coach helping work less hours and make more money! Business Coach for Entrepreneurs

The easiest way to think about this is to answer the question, what does my client get AFTER they have done business with me? What do they feel, think or say after you have delivered your product or service to them? Think about the benefits to the client and focus on that in your headline.

In summary your professional Headline should feature your main keyword twice, the earlier in the headline the better. It must read well ie. not look like it's stuffed full of keywords and the same keyword must also feature in your summary.

Tip 4 – Your Photograph

Sam was once asked to introduce a connection of a good business contact to one of her best clients. As she always does, she went to check the person's profile out on LinkedIn. The first thing she saw was the photograph. It was of a scruffy looking man, in a string vest in his garden! This was a person looking to be connected with her number one multinational corporate client, and yet he chose that photograph to appear on his business profile.

It sounds obvious, I know, but your professional photograph should be exactly that... professional. In a smart business suit, regardless of your trade or profession and taken by a professional photographer, preferably with a friendly and inviting picture. You only get one chance to make an impression on LinkedIn.

Tip 5 – Your Public URL

Your public URL is the small blue link that appears at the bottom of your LinkedIn profile. This is generated by LinkedIn and quite often contains random numbers and letters. You can edit this to make it match your name or business name. Change the public URL to your name or your name and business name.

Tip 6 –How to Use Your Public Profile

Once you have a public URL you are happy with, you can then use this link to drive visits and connections from your email signature, your website, your business card and other social media channels. If you are just starting out in business and don't have a website yet, you can use this link to give people a place to learn more about you and your business.

Tip 7 – Your Professional Summary

This is the section directly underneath your photograph and contact details. You can add a summary about you and your business, this is under-utilised by many business owners on LinkedIn. A general structure for building your LinkedIn summary is below. Keep it to 2-3 sentences per paragraph. Make a great first impression.

Paragraph 1 – About the Company and your Role in the business

Paragraph 2 – Key Benefits, What you Deliver to Clients and what makes you different – make it very clear why your target market should do business with you

Paragraph 3 – What you are passionate about

Paragraph 4 – Additional Activities such as Community Work or any Volunteering that you do.

Paragraph 5 – Awards and Achievements

Paragraph 6 – Specialities: AKA a list of keywords to help you get found

Your profile should ooze credibility, and this will help you appear as someone who is serious about their business and someone that they should connect to.

Tip 8 – Your Experience

The section covering your previous positions and jobs is important because it allows LinkedIn to suggest potential connections for you based on where you have worked before. Make sure you complete this but don't write a novel under each heading, just a few lines.

Tip 9 – Add Skills to Your Profile

LinkedIn allows you to add Skills to your profile which you can then be endorsed for, the trick with skills is to keep it to the skills that you actually want to be endorsed for, so you probably have 100 different skills that you are good at to some extent, if you want to be credible and get known for being great in a particular area then restrict your skills list to 25 or 30 core skills that you would be happy for someone to endorse you for.

Also bear in mind that skills you once had may not be relevant to what you do now, so always keep this list up to date and add or remove skills from time to time. This list will be used by people in their searches for people with relevant skills, it is a tool most useful for recruiters and head-hunters, less relevant for business owners, however it is important that you list skills and that you can then be endorsed by others for having those skills.

Tip 10 – Add Rich Content & Media to your Profile

At the time of writing this book, LinkedIn is gradually rolling out the ability to add videos, links and documents to your LinkedIn Profile. When you go into 'Edit Profile' you will now see a plus '+' button next to the edit tools, and this allows you to add a link to a video for example a YouTube or Vimeo video, or a link to your blog or a landing page. You could also include a PDF brochure or PowerPoint presentation about your Product or Service.

This will really bring your profile to life and give people the opportunity to explore your business and professional profile in more detail. The phasing out of this relatively new ability to add rich content to your profile is expected to be completed by the end of 2013. Don't worry if your profile won't allow you yet, keep checking in and make sure you add some great content when your profile allows you to.

Tip 11 – Add Publications to Your Profile

If you have written and published books, articles, papers etc. then you can now add these to your profile. If your publication is available online you can add links to your profile to drive sales, this is one way to give you books more exposure. In addition, publishing papers or articles raises your credibility so you will be positioning yourself as an expert in your field the more publications you have that you can link through your profile.

Tip 12 – Add Voluntary Experience to Your Profile

When people look at your profile, most of what they read is all about you as a business professional. After all, LinkedIn is a business networking platform, however you can add some personal details to your profile which contain details of your philanthropic work, or voluntary work raising awareness for causes and charities that you support. If you are involved in any voluntary or community work you can share this on your LinkedIn profile, if you have a JustGiving.com account then why not add this to your voluntary section and use LinkedIn as an additional way to raise funds.

Tip 13 – Link Twitter to your Profile

You can easily link your LinkedIn profile to your Twitter account(s). You will develop more followers this way, you can choose to post your Status Updates via Twitter, directly from LinkedIn. Ensure that you link your Twitter accounts to LinkedIn.

Tip 14 – Use Calls to Action on to Your Web Links

When you are adding your website to your LinkedIn profile, the standard way to do this is within the 'Edit Contact Details' section of your profile. Most people use LinkedIn's standard drop-down box which includes 'Personal Website', 'Company Website', 'Blog' etc. These are pretty boring descriptions and everyone uses them on LinkedIn.

They do not really entice someone to want to click on the link though. There is a different way to add your website to any link that you want, and be able to include a 'Call to Action'. Instead of choosing 'Company Website' from the drop down menu, choose 'Other'. LinkedIn will then give you a short space to write some text, and then a new place to add your link. So here are some examples:

Old Description: Blog

New Description: Click for top Business Tips
(where the link goes to your blog page)

Old Description: Company Website
New Description: For great value Hosting Packages
(where the link goes to your products page)

Old Description: Personal Website
New Description: Get your FREE special report
(where the link goes to a landing opt-in page)

Tip 15 – Add a Phone Number and Email to your profile

It sounds obvious, that you would want people to make contact with you once they have found you on LinkedIn, however many people still miss this vital element of your profile. Make sure that you at least have an email address for business and a phone number for your office. From the LinkedIn smartphone App people can make a call to you directly from within your LinkedIn profile.

15 Tips to Grow Your Connections to 500+

LinkedIn = Connections at 500+

LinkedOut = less than 500 connections

We deliver 'LinkedIn or LinkedOut?' workshops all over the world on the benefit and value of LinkedIn and more importantly for business owners, sales teams and in-house recruiters, we show delegates how to be successful through mastering LinkedIn.

The most common questions that comes up at almost every training or workshop, is around the subject of connections or 'Contacts' as LinkedIn is now referring to them as. We are going to tackle each of the common questions that arise here:

Why should I grow my network to 500+?

This question comes back to the VCP Process®. Having 500+ connections gives you great visibility, the more visibility you have and the more people you are connected to, the higher chance that your profile will be viewed and that someone will want to do business with you. Business people like to be connected to people who are well connected, so you will naturally draw attention to yourself if you are a 500+ LinkedIn user. Once you hit 500+ LinkedIn will not show how many connections you have, in a way it does give you some credibility, if you are connected to 500+ people then the perception is that you must know a lot of people and have some considerable influence. You are more likely going to receive connection requests from other people when you are at 500+, which equals less work for you in growing your network, it will grow organically.

Another reason for wanting to be 500+ as an initial goal, is that the more 1st connections you have the higher chance that you are going to be able to reach your target market. When we look at Advanced Searches later in this book, you will really start to see the value of having a high number, 500+ network. When you run a search in LinkedIn, you are effectively only going to see 1st, 2nd and 3rd connections, the more 1st connections you have the more likely that your search results will yield the name of the person you want to do business with or reveal connections that can help you get into your dream client company.

Should I connect with people I don't know?

We recommend that you accept every connection request, even if you do not know the person. If you really want to generate new business from LinkedIn you do need to be connected to a high number of people on LinkedIn, even if you don't know the person directly, their LinkedIn network could lead you to a massive contract or could offer up a dream 2nd or 3rd connection that you would never have been able to see before. LinkedIn is different to Facebook, you are not posting personal pictures of you having fun at the weekend or revealing things that people would otherwise not be able to find out about you elsewhere.

LinkedIn is a business networking platform, online. You never know why someone is asking for you to connect with them that you don't know, it could be that they want to do business with you, having read your amazing profile! You can always remove them from your contacts if the way they go about their updates or relationship building is not for you. Bear in mind that most people on LinkedIn are business professionals, just because you connect with someone you don't know today, it does not mean that they can do anything to you or your business, the more connections you have the more useful your LinkedIn network can be to you.

The decision around whether you connect to people on LinkedIn who you do not know is of course personal choice, just bear in mind all of the benefits that go with having a strong and large network before making the choice to restrict your network to people you know personally. It is also very easy to block, report or remove a connection that you accept and no longer want to have in your network.

The next 15 points all relate to growing your LinkedIn Connections, these are easy and simple things you can do to increase your online network and at the same time improve your visibility and credibility, which you know by now will help you move into profitable relationships.

Tip 16 – Connect with Clients

One of the easiest way to build your connections is to connect with all of your current and previous clients. Even if you have not done business with someone for a while, it's a good way to re-engage with them and re-kindle the relationship. This alone should help to get you closer to 500+ connections.

Tip 17 – Connect with Suppliers

Your supplier's networks are invaluable. As a customer of the business if you asked for help in securing a connection I am sure that they would be happy to help. They want to keep you as a customer and are more than likely to connect with you and more importantly, facilitate introductions to other people in their network.

Tip 18 – Connect with Ex-Colleagues

A Business Coach in the UK, Andrew came on one of our LinkedIn Masterclass courses in 2011. We talked about the benefits of connecting with people you used to work with, ex-collegues, team members, managers, subordinates. During that course he reconnected with an ex-colleague of 15 years previous, they had worked together at Unilever. That one connection he made transformed his business and in 2012, that one connection was worth 75% of his turnover last year. It has since spun off into more business for more of Andrew's business contacts and all of this happened because of LinkedIn.

These dormant connections, people who you may not have dealt with in the last 4 or 5 years, will have a strong affinity with you, want to help you providing you have always got on well in the past and in the last 4 or 5 years will have been building an amazing network themselves which could be of use to you and vice versa. It is always worthwhile touching base with ex-colleagues.

Tip 19 – Toplinked.com

Visit TopLinked.com, and register with a free account. This will add you to a list of people who are willing to be invited by others that want to grow a strong network. This will increase the number of times you are invited to connect by other people.

In addition you will receive regular updates from TopLinked.com with lists of people who are happy to be invited to connect, even if you do not know them. Using this list can increase your number of connections very quickly. One colleague of Sam's in the recruitment sector, established 2000+ new connections in less than 24hours!

Tip 20 – Connect with your Staff

If you run a business with a team, then ensure that you connect with each of your staff. There are a number of reasons for this, firstly you can see who they are connecting with and be ahead of the game if they suddenly start connecting with recruiters or head-hunters! However the main benefit is that you can train your entire team how to use LinkedIn effectively and replicate your VCP way beyond your own capabilities. If you were to add up all of the connections that you have and then add to this the 1st connections of your own team, you can just imagine the online footprint that you could generate across LinkedIn.

The great thing about networking is that everyone's network is unique, each of your team bring a different background, education, work history and you never know who they know that could be a business-changing contact! Make sure that the team have a similar message on their profile about your business, so that if a potential client visited your profile and then one of your team's you would be able to see the same professional message about what you deliver for your clients. Encourage them to spend time on LinkedIn and this will all help the business to move the relationships online through the VCP Process®.

Tip 21 – Connect with Group Members

When you go to connect with someone new, LinkedIn gives you options to choose how you know the person. When you read this section you will see that we are recommending that you connect with people that today, you may not know. Often the challenge comes when you see someone you really want to connect with, yet they seem unreachable because tey are 3rd connections of out of your network.

This simple tip will help you to connect with any person you want through LinkedIn. When you find someone on LinkedIn that you do not know and you really want to connect with them, scroll down to the bottom of their LinkedIn profile and you will see a list of all of the Groups that the person is a member of. Choose a group that they are in and join it yourself.

Once you are a member of the same group, a new option to connect will be shown. When you request a connection, a new option under 'How do you know [person's name]?' comes up. You will now see the word 'Groups' show up in the list. Choose 'Groups' from the drop down menu, select the group that you mutually share and then click on Connect.

Always make sure that you personalise the message. Never ever sell, but do make sure that you either compliment them or mention something you have in common.

Some useful phrases to use in a Connection Request message:

"I saw that we are in the same LinkedIn group together and have similar interests."

"I saw that we have 23 mutual connections and I thought it would be of interest to connect"

"I read your article on [insert subject], and would really like to connect with you."

"I watched your presentation on [insert subject] and thought you made some really relevant points, it was really fantastic!"

These are simple phrases that work when requesting a connection from someone you don't know.

Tip 22 – Connect with Friends & Family

Connecting with friends and family can sometimes reveal some interesting facts about people who you have known for years, especially your extended family. Connect with your parents, grandparents, sisters, brothers, uncles, aunts, cousins and you just never know what opportunities are going to come up.

At most family gatherings you are completely focused on the family, children, personal things, but imagine coming back into a work environment to discover that one of your close family members actually knows the person you have been trying to land as a client for weeks. It is an obvious one, but not everyone does this. You just might be surprised!

Tip 23 – Connect with School, College and University Contacts

You never know where your past colleagues are now working, you also don't know who they know. It can be so much fun going back over the old college year books and into the Alumni groups on LinkedIn to find people who you used to hang out with at School, College or University.

Some will be running their own businesses, some will be climbing the career ladder in large companies, you just never know where they are and how you can help them and vice versa. One of the people who recently attended one of our LinkedIn courses just told me that she reconnected with an old school friend and has just landed her first international client as a result. This tip is useful and also fun!

Tip 24 – Use LinkedIn's 'People You May Know' feature

LinkedIn is highly intuitive, this amazing business networking platform knows who you are already connected to and your extended network, and because you have provided data about your past history both for work and schools, it can easily connect you with people that you might know based on a combination of these elements. The 'People You May Know' section appears in multiple places within LinkedIn, always on your Home Page. Use this to seek out people that are most likely to accept your invitation, people you already have a connection with.

Tip 25 – Connect with people you meet at Networking Events

This can be done whilst you are at the event itself, using the LinkedIn App, or you can do this when you return to your office. Look at the business cards you collected at the event and go through them, do a people search on LinkedIn for their name and ask them to connect. Always personalise the message mentioning the event you attended and any other comments related to your discussion at the event. You could suggest a coffee or follow up meeting. It's a great way to connect your face to face networking with your online activity. It means you can always stay in touch with your contacts through LinkedIn.

Tip 26 – Connect with all of the business cards you have in or on your desk

I am sure if you are like most business owners, that you have a stack of business cards either on your desk or hidden in a drawer or a box somewhere. Each of these business cards represents someone you have once met and exchanged cards with. By connecting with each of these people you are creating another touch point with these contacts and may rekindle some business relationships that you had not kept up to date with.

Just by adding each person whose business card you are holding onto you could add significant connections to your total LinkedIn network.

Tip 27 – Connect with Speakers at Conferences

The great thing about Conferences is that whether you attended or not, the Speaker does not actually know if you were in the audience. The Conferences for the industry that you are targeting will often profile keynote speakers on the before, during and after communication at the event.

If you simply send a nice email to a speaker, telling them how brilliant you thought their presentation was at the [insert conference name] event, then they will always connect with you.

We do this successfully with people in the industry or profession that we want to target, it works because you have common ground, plus you are brushing the ego which is always a good approach when you are looking for someone to connect with you.

Tip 28 – Connect with people you meet at Trade Shows & Exhibitions

Trade Shows and Exhibitions are a great place to meet people. You can visit 50+ stands in one day and usually there are business cards available to pick up at each stand. Talk to people on the stand when you go, find out more about the company and then connect with the people you meet when you get back to your office.

Tip 29 – Connect with Thought Leaders in your Industry

Regardless of the industry you are in, there will be key players globally that speak and write in your industry. You can typically find these people by researching your topic on the internet. TED talks is a great place to find Thought Leaders, you can brush the ego when approaching these people, when you ask them to connect mention how much you were inspired by their talk, their presentation or what they said.

Tip 30 – Connect with people that Inspire You

If you are reading this book, then you are most likely to be interested in improving your business in some way. Any business book that inspires you, connect with the Author and ask them to connect with you, you'll be surprised, people genuinely want to be in touch with their followers and will usually connect with a fan. If you are inspired by a Business Leader, Mentor, speaker or Author then just ask, the worst that can happen is that they choose not to connect.

You can connect with Sam Rathling here:
http://ie.linkedin.com/in/samrathling

You can connect with Derek Reilly here:
http://ie.linkedin.com/in/derekreilly

10 Tips for LinkedIn Status Updates

LinkedIn = Proactively Using Status Updates

LinkedOut = Never posting articles, blogs or updates

Tip 31 -Use Status Updates to thank other people

Giving gratitude is a great way to help others and thank people in your network for the great support that they have been to you. Use your Status Updates on LinkedIn to do this, and mention them in your comments, as well as adding a link to their website or blog. This is an easy way to bring content your network and to share with people that you give to others by saying thank you.

Tip 32 - Use Status Updates to share Success Stories

Share any company success stories, so share information about what you are up to, that is relevant to your business but without selling.

For example:

"Just back from a great client meeting, where they told me they have saved 75% of their recruitment costs since working with us! I love saving people money and helping them to cut their admin time."

"Another happy customer just sent the whole office a box of chocolates, balloons and a gorgeous thank you card. We are so privileged to have such fantastic clients."

"Another client has decided to come on board with us, we are really looking forward to helping them to look after all of their printing needs, a great day and the business continues to grow."

"We are delighted to celebrate Julia's 6th year in the business with us! A happy and motivated team here and we love passing that energy and great service on to our clients".

"Just back from training an amazing group of Entrepreneurs on how to get the most value from LinkedIn."

It's a clever way to say what you do and how you do it but without selling to your contacts, it is a subtle and indirect way of letting people know what you do and how you add value.

Tip 33 - Use Status Updates to create 'buzz' about your Business

If you want people in your network to notice you and your company create content that is viral, engaging, interesting and will give you massive visibility. You can easily create buzz especially if you combine this with other forms of social media. You could run a competition, engage with your followers and connections, use the status updates to post landing pages, excite people about an upcoming event or spread positivity about your brand, your business and your success. This will get you noticed and the Status Updates are a place to do this.

Tip 34 - Use Status Updates to drive visits to your website

You can post links to any website in the Status Updates from the LinkedIn home page, so use this opportunity to drive traffic to your website. If you want to be able to track the effectiveness of this then use a free tool such as bit.ly: http://bit.ly .

Simply create a free account on a website such as bit.ly and then paste a link there to a web page, landing page or blog that you have created. The bit.ly link will be a short-link which you can add into LinkedIn updates or Twitter or Facebook. From this every time someone clicks on the link it will be tracked. Then you can 'View Stats' and see how many clicks came through LinkedIn.

When you are posting a link that you have created, it is important that it is useful content and not a sales pitch, people on LinkedIn don't like to be sold to.

Tip 35 - Deliver Engaging Content to Your Target Market

When you post Status Updates always have your customer in mind. Who is your target market, if you are B2B (business to business), what is the job title of the buyer in a company that you would like to do business with? Is it the HR Manager, the Purchasing Manager, the IT Manager? Is the CEO or Managing Director? What industry is that potential customer in? Think about what they like to read, think about articles that they would find of interest. Then simply go to the LinkedIn Today news feed and follow the industry or profession that would appeal to your target market.

If you are B2C (business to consumer), ie. That you are selling to the general public, think about demographics, does your product or service appeal to parents of young children, first time homebuyers, recently retired couples? Are you selling in the local market or internationally? Either way, whatever the demographic and location is, get into their mind and think like them, what content would they like to read or feel appealing?

The most recent activity shows on your LinkedIn profile, so as an example, let's say you were targeting HR Manager, and you really wanted them to connect with you. You would find a very relevant article on LinkedIn, such as "8 Ways to Drive Employee Engagement in Your Organisation". This is very topical for HR departments at the moment, so you are going to ask an HR Manager to connect with you. They are naturally going to check out your profile before deciding whether to do business with you.

So the HR Manager of a large company you would like to do business with comes to your profile, following your connection request. They read your very credible headline and a profile written to impress HR people. They then see an article that helps them called "8 Ways to Drive Employee Engagement in Your Organisation". They are going to recognise you as someone who knows about their industry and are more likely to connect with you after seeing your profile because you clearly are in tune with their industry, and if you posted that article you'd like to see more.

You are increasing the chances of your target market connecting with you by making your Status Updates relevant to the people you want to do business with. Your visibility and credibility will go up massively with these people if done well.

Tip 36 - Use Status Updates to share Videos

When you share a status update which has not been generated from the LinkedIn Today section, you can choose to place a link into the update you are sharing. If you use video in your business, or you wish to share videos created by other people, then you can easily place a link to a YouTube or Vimeo video to share with your network.

Simply find the video you want to share, for example a YouTube video, then choose the option to 'Share'. This will show a unique URL for the video, simply copy the link and come back into LinkedIn, create a new update and then paste the link into the update. A screen shot of the video will be created and then you can comment on the video before sharing with your network.

Tip 37 - Use Status Updates to share your latest Blogs

When you write a blog it is important that you use a catchy headline so that people are more inclined to click on it, as well as thinking about optimising the headline for search engines. LinkedIn is a great place to share your latest blog. Use headings for your blogs that people are most likely to enter into a search and that would encourage someone from your LinkedIn network to read more. Start with headlines such as:

"How To..."

"8 Different Ways To..."

"10 Tips for..."

"The Best Advice for..."

If you want some great ideas, see what other people are writing about in the LinkedIn Today section. Once you have created your blog post, simply place a link to the blog in the Status Update at the top of your Home Page on LinkedIn.

If you have never created a blog before and want some help then this is the best article (over 7100 words) on how to set one up. http://dukeo.com/how-to-start-a-blog/. If you have never come across Dukeo before then it is a blog well worth following.

Tip 38 - Use Status Updates Frequently

Every time you post an update, you appear in the LinkedIn Activity Feed which any of your connections would see on their home page. Don't worry, they don't get a message every time you post something, they will only see it at that moment in time if they are logged in on their computer or on the LinkedIn App on the phone. Your frequency of posting will drive more profile views and we recommend as an absolute minimum that you post content once a day although 3-4 times a day will give you more visibility.

If the content you are posting is good and useful, then your credibility will also be boosted. You will notice that more people want to connect to you and you will drive engagement by people posting, liking and sharing what you have posted in your updates.

Tip 39 - Use Status Updates to Promote Other People

You can always mention others in your updates. This is agreat way to profile other people in your network. It's the same feature that Facebook has for their updates, if you mention their name then your contact will appear and you can link them to the update. Reasons you may want to do this are to showcase the other person, recommend the other person or talk about them in a nice way. All of this would be seen as helpful and giving to the other person and would come back to you in some way. You could say "Just back from a fantastic meeting with Derek Reilly, he has fantastic offers on business cards at the moment, so if you're running low then I highly recommend you speak with Derek for a great deal."

Tip 40 – Theme Some Of Your Status Updates

Frequency is key, when it comes to sending out content over your LinkedIn network that gets you noticed. Theming your Status

Updates can be a great way to remember to post and to keep your message on track. For example you could come up with specific names for each day of the week that fit with your business:

- **Monday Madness** –this would include posting a strange or funny post or article on your news feed that would grab attention.

- **Tips on Tuesday** – This would give free tips to people to show your expertise.

- **Win on Wednesday** - this would be the day to share success, talk about a recent win in the business either for the whole company, or one of your tem

- **Thursday Trivia** – Engaging your network with questions is a good way to get responses by having them guess the answer to a question relevant to your industry

- **Friday Feature** – This is the day you could promote someone else in your network and feature them and their business

If you create your own theme you will find it easier to post something and stay on track, but once you have started don't forget to keep it up. You could also do something similar on Facebook and Twitter.

10 Tips for Finding, Approaching & Managing Contacts

LinkedIn = Using Advanced Searches to Proactively Find and Contact People

LinkedOut = Being Reactive and never using Advanced Searches

Regardless of the number of connections you have today, your network is going to do one thing consistently and that is, GROW!

Even if you are purely reactive on LinkedIn you will be receiving contact requests and this in turn will increase the number of overall people in your network. If you really want to benefit from LinkedIn in your business, it is important that you understand how to search for People, Companies and Groups. It is also important that you know how to manage your contacts and keep on top of your ever-growing contact base.

This section of the book is all about finding, approaching and managing your connections. Once you know how to do this you can really start to see the massive value that LinkedIn can bring to you and if applicable, to your team.

Searching LinkedIn works in a very similar way to searching on Google. The more specific you are the better. If you know the person's name and company or name and location (country) then put both in as quite often with over 200 million members even a name search will come up with many results. The trick is knowing how to find people and then finding a way to connect with them, either through a mutual shared interest or connection.

The next section of tips covers the many types of advanced searches you can do on LinkedIn to help you to identify potential customers, and then we also cover how you can manage and track these contacts on Linkedin.

Tip 41 - Use Advanced Searches to find people in your Locality

If you want to find people who are local to you, then you simply go into the search bar at the top of the page and type in the name of your town or city. People with this location on their profile will be shown in the search results. From there you can see who is your 1st connection (already connected to you), 2nd connection (1 connection away from you, you have a mutually shared contact), or 3 connection (2 degrees of separation from you).

If you prefer to look for people by country instead of by town or city, then click on the 'Advanced Search' link to the right of the main search bar on top of every LinkedIn page and choose a country from the list. If your country is not listed then you can start typing the first few letters of the country and LinkedIn will suggest a country from the list. Choose the country and click on search and all of the search results will be people who are based in your chosen country.

Tip 42 - Use Advanced Searches to find the names of people who buy your Product/Service

You should have a pretty good idea by now on the typical buyers for your product or service. We spoke in the last section about the importance of providing engaging content for you contacts, now you can use the Advanced Searches to actually look for them.

If you want to look for a Job Title or a key phrase then you need to use speech marks around the phrase to make the search exactly what you are looking for. For example:

HR Manager Putting this search into LinkedIn will mean that all of the LinkedIn profiles that contain both the word HR and the word Manager, literally hundreds and thousands of profiles will come up.

"HR Manager" If you do the same search again, only this time with the key phrase in speech marks then only profiles with the full phrase "HR Manager" will appear.

You can also use a string of keywords and phrases to include the words OR, AND or AND NOT. For example you could search "HR Manager" OR "HR Director" AND NOT "HR Assistant".

There are many tricks you can use with LinkedIn searches, this is quite advanced and typically used in the recruitment industry. You can learn more about this here, also known as 'Boolean Strings':

Glen Cathey has a great website that he runs called "The Boolean Black Belt: http://www.booleanblackbelt.com/

Also, there is a very good video about Boolean search by Jonathan Campbell available here:

http://www.socialtalent.co/resources/?page_id=886

The password for the video is **r3d2kn1plg**

Tip 43 - Use Advanced Searches to find Introducers of your Product/Service

So in tip 42, we looked at how to search for your end client and prospective buyers. In this tip we are going to focus on 'Introducers' or 'Referral Partners'. These are companies or people who sell to the same target market as you, but offer something different than you. The best way to think about this, is to look at who else is regularly servicing your target market.

Find people in professions or categories that you know you would be able to give referrals to if you built up a strong relationship. Some examples are below of the kind of Referral Partners or Introducers for various industries:

Profession:	Good Referral Partners:
Photographer	Jeweller, Travel Agent, Videographer, Bridal Shop, Wedding Planner
Plumber	Builder, Electrician, Roofer, Plasterer, Architect, Engineer
Recruitment	Human Resources Consultant, Business Coach, Accountant, Printer, Training Company
Accountant	Solicitor, Financial Advisor, Bank Manager, Business Coach
Web Designer	Copywriter, Marketing Agency, Graphic Designer, Printer, Promotional Products

Think about what type of referral partners would be right for your business. Then start researching these using LinkedIn. Apply the same search techniques that we have already talked about and use the keywords and key phrases. Then narrow and refine your search to your locality and you'll start to find good people to partner with to help you reach multiple end clients.

Tip 44 – Use Company Searches to find dream Prospects

If you are looking to specifically work with a large company, then use the Company Search by typing in the company name and selecting their LinkedIn Company Page. Then on the right hand side, you will see how you are connected to this prospect client. Once you can see who can get you in there you can start to use these techniques in this section to help you to get closer to the buyers of your products and services.

Tip 45 - Personalise all Connection Requests

When you ask a person to connect with you, the standard LinkedIn message will appear, as follows:

I'd like to add you to my professional network on LinkedIn.

- [Your Name]

Our recommendation is that when you connect to a new person, that you always personalise the message by using their first name and customising the message to give a short introduction. It can be useful to mention your mutual connections, a shared group or interest, or something impressive about their profile. This will increase the chances of them saying 'Yes' I'll connect.

Tip 46 – Use the 'Get Introduced' option

When you find a LinkedIn Profile that you would like to connect to, you have the option of choosing how to connect to the person. Some people allow you to send an 'InMail', if you want to pay LinkedIn for a premium account then you will be able to freely send InMails to people.

If you prefer to ask for an introduction then you can use LinkedIn's option to 'Get Introduced'. This is relevant when a person is a 2nd of 3rd connection to you.

Tip 47 – See how you are connected to 2nd and 3rd connections

When you see your search results a list of people will appear, and then you can see which of them are 1st, 2nd and 3rd connections. When someone in the list is a 2nd or 3rd connection, you will see a Green link underneath their name, with "XX Shared Connections". When you click on this link, LinkedIn will show you all of the people that you could use to help facilitate an introduction.

Dependent on the level of relationship you have with these mutual contacts, you can either pick up the phone to a shared connection and ask for help, you could message the person through LinkedIn to ask how well they know the person or you could simply ask for the connection directly by sending a personalised connection request.

This feature is very useful when you go to meet a new contact face to face, before the meeting go through their LinkedIn connections and ask for help in the meeting if you feel comfortable and this will help you to connect to 2nd and 3rd connections. It will help by you sharing your contacts first, if you help the other person first with your connections, they will be more inclined to want to share theirs with you.

Tip 48 – Get to people who seem unreachable by joining LinkedIn Groups

We'll talk about groups in a later section, but an easy way to reach people who seem unreachable and out of your network, or 3rd connections is to scroll to the bottom of their profile. You will then see a list of all of the LinkedIn groups that they are a member of. Simply click on the Group and join that group. Once accepted to that new group, you can send a connection request to the person, and when asked by LinkedIn to confirm how you know the person, you choose 'We are in the same Group' from the drop down menu, and find the group. Your newly joined Group will appear in the list. This way you never need to know their email address or say that 'We've done Business together' when you clearly have not.

Tip 49 - Back Up Your Connections by Exporting all Data from LinkedIn

When you go into the connections or contacts part of LinkedIn, scroll down to the bottom of the page and on the bottom right you will see a very small blue link which reads 'Export Connections'. This allows you to export your data into a .CSV file which is a type of Excel file. Once you have exported the data you will see on your Excel file all of the data from your connections which includes contact details, names and country as well as any other information taken from the profile.

This tip is useful for a couple of reasons:

1. This is a good way to back up all of your LinkedIn data. If something ever happened to your LinkedIn account or you were ever blocked from using your account by LinkedIn, which has happened to a good friend of mine, then you could stand to lose all of the connections you have spent years building up. Repeat this exercise once per month and keep a back-up of your connections.

2. Now you have all of your LinkedIn connections in one place, you can use this list in a number of ways. You can create an opt-in mailing list using software such as Mailchimp, Aweber or Constant Contact. When you do this be sure to always include an 'unsubscribe' option and indicate that you have their email address

as a valued connection on LinkedIn. This will ensure that you comply with anti-spam regulation and data protection.

3. You can now export all of these connections into your database of contacts, there are many CRM systems on the market, some available for a small business from as little as €4.00 per month, I would recommend Salesforce.com but you can research which is best for your business.

Tip 50 - Categorise your Contacts by 'Tagging' them

The new version of LinkedIn Contacts makes it easier than ever to 'tag' your contacts or connections. Each person you know on LinkedIn as a 1st connection can be 'tagged', which essentially puts an identification flag on them so you can group your contacts into a particular category. For example, you might want to tag all of your 'Clients', 'Suppliers', 'Partners', 'Friends', 'Family' etc. and then you can send a group message to these people as a tagged group.

If you prefer to tag people by the frequency of contact that you need to have with them, then you may want to tag contacts as simply, A, B, C, D. Where your 'A' contacts are your top contacts that you need to keep weekly or bi-weekly contact with and as you move down to B and C contacts, the frequency would be less. This of course depends on your type of business and how you would like to manage your contacts. The point here is that really it is up to you how you make and keep contact with your connections, tagging provides a simple system that allows you to keep on top of your ever-growing network. Just remember to keep your messages send to tagged groups to a minimum as they cannot be personalised within LinkedIn, and it is very obvious when someone has sent out a blast email. And always remember to provide useful and engaging content, and never ever sell!

10 Tips for your LinkedIn Company Profile

LinkedIn = Company Profile 100% Complete

LinkedOut = No Company Profile Set Up

Tip 51 – Create a Great Company Page

Like Facebook and other social media sites, LinkedIn now has dedicated Company Pages. Take the time to set one up rather than having a company in the personal profile pages section. You can do this by simply going to Company Section of LinkedIn and choosing 'Add a Company' from the top right hand corner.

Tip 52 – Allocate Time to Content Creation and Sourcing of Great Material

Before you start a company page, be sure that you will have the time to keep it updated with "fresh" content. A stale page is probably worse than no page at all. You or someone in your team needs to responsible for keeping the page updated, delivering great content and information that is worthy of someone following the company.

Tip 53 – Build up Your Company Followers

A Company Page helps LinkedIn members learn about your business, brand, products and services, and job opportunities. Any LinkedIn member can follow a company page. The more followers you have, the more visibility your brand will have. Set realistic goals for your followers, only really big brand names and well known, listed companies would be able to reach millions of followers, so don't expect miracles and build this up gradually. You could start by asking your clients, suppliers, friends and family who you are connected to on LinkedIn to follow you.

Tip 54 – Add all of your Products and Services

This is a simple but important task, you can now create a page for each of your Products and Services within your LinkedIn Company Page. Each page can feature text, links to videos, links to documents and web pages as well as being able to add keywords, key information and recommendations for these Products and Services. You can simply copy and paste the information from your website, or if you don't have a website, then use the LinkedIn Company Page as your new website until you are ready to create one.

Tip 55 – Use the Analytics Tools provided by LinkedIn

Don't forget to check your analytics tab to see who is visiting your page, following your company and engaging in your conversations. This will help you to measure the success of your Company Page, also look at how many followers you have, and who those followers are. These are potential prospects, you could also send a nice message to thank them for following your Company.

Tip 56 – Make Sure that Your Email Matches Your Domain Name

Currently, companies without their own distinct email domain (e.g., yourcompany.com) can't create a Company Page, because it's not possible to use email domains such as hotmail.com, gmail.com, or other generic email providers. If you don't have a distinct email domain, you might create a group to promote your company instead.

Tip 57 – Keep Your Staff List Up To Date

Company Pages are designed to display current and former employees, alumni, or new hires. Only current employees should appear on your Company Page's landing page. If a LinkedIn member is associating themselves with your company page and they shouldn't be you have to send a specific request to LinkedIn stating the reasons why they are to be removed.

Tip 58 – Keep the Information Your Company Shares Relevant

We recommend that company status updates stay authentic, relevant, and short. The better your content, the greater the chance it goes viral through likes, shares, and comments. Posts that feel like spam will not get shared and, in fact, could result in your business losing followers.

Tip 59 – Attract the best Talent to your Company

Upgrading to a Silver or Gold Career Page gives you access to a full suite of features for promoting careers at your company, including a clickable banner, customizable modules, analytics on who is viewing the page, direct links to recruiters, video content, and more. With a Gold Career Page, you can customize up to five different versions of the page to show different content based on the viewer's LinkedIn profile. This would be more relevant for larger companies with a headcount in excess of 50 staff.

Tip 60 The Importance of a Great Company Cover and Image

Have a well-designed / engaging /original cover profile picture for your company page. You want to be remembered and for LinkedIn members to follow your company. Also remember that you will be uploading a Standard Logo and Square Logo for your company. Make sure that you preview these once uploaded so that they look correct.

It is important that your company image is royalty and copyright free. You can use this website to get good stock photography for free: http://sxc.hu. You can search using keywords and find images that best suit what you do, if you prefer there are plenty of paid images you could use also.

Here is the information taken from the LinkedIn Help Center in relation to image uploads for a Company Page. If you're a Company Page administrator, you can upload a homepage image or logo. The file requirements are:

Image - Minimum 646x220 pixels, PNG/JPEG/GIF format, Maximum 2 MB

Logo - 100x60 pixels, PNG/JPEG/GIF format, Maximum 2 MB

To upload the image or logo:

- Create your image file. You can crop larger images after uploading, if necessary.

- Click *Edit* at the top of your Company Page homepage.

- Locate the *Image* or *Logo* section and click the *Add image* link or *Edit* (whichever is present).

- Click *Upload* to attach your image file, and then click *Save*.

- Click *Publish* in the top right of the page.

Note: If your image won't upload, make sure that your image is the correct size or slightly larger. Images that are smaller will not upload. Since the pages were designed to use an image that's wider than taller, make sure the image is the correct orientation.

If the image has the correct size and dimensions shown above, here's what you can do:

Solution 1: Save your file as a PNG file and then try uploading it again.

Solution 2: Clear your browser cookies, sign back in to your account, and then try uploading it again.

Solution 3: Use a different Internet browser to sign in to your account and try uploading it again.

10 Tips for LinkedIn Recommendations

LinkedIn = At least 10 great Recommendations for current role/company

LinkedOut = Less than 10 Recommendations for what you do

Recommendations are all about credibility, they are social proof that you are good at what you do and that other people should also buy from you. The more you have on your profile the more chance that someone will decide to do business with you. The beauty of LinkedIn recommendations is that everyone can see who has endorsed you.

If you run a business this is fantastic, because a potential client can read great stories about how you helped other clients all on your LinkedIn personal page or your LinkedIn Company page. It's worth investing some time in getting the right kind of recommendations as every time you do get a recommendation, it will appear on your contacts' home feeds and will give you additional visibility.

Every time you give a recommendation you are helping another person, this giving activity is a great way to build relationships, motivate your network to want to help you back and build greater credibility. You are really taking your relationship building to the next level when you focus on recommending others, as it means that your level of trust with those people is high.

Tip 61 – Give Recommendations to Suppliers

When you recommend a supplier to your business, you are in effect motivating that person to give you a better service, prioritising you over other contacts and helping them to know who to focus on. If a supplier is good at what they do and you go and give them a surprise recommendation it is a very powerful way to give. This giving activity will result in your supplier going above and beyond and when you need a new connection or if you ask for their help in getting into one of their customers, they are more inclined to do it because you already helped their business.

It is a nice thing to do, giving a recommendation to a supplier, as you are building the relationship to take it from a client/supplier position to a position of let's see how we can help each other with introductions etc. Your suppliers will often be in and out of companies that you would love to work with, so do not underestimate their network and the value it could be to you.

Tip 62 – Give Recommendations to Clients

Recommending clients or people that you have worked with in client companies, is a really powerful way to retain customers, keep them happy and go above and beyond. If you are recommending their company to others and you want to maintain that business and make yourself irreplaceable to the customer, then this is a great way to cement a relationship. Your only goal with every customer is to make yourself so valuable to that organisation that even if someone else came along offering another solution that they would not change because they have you and you look after them so well that it would be impossible for them to go elsewhere. Recommendations are one tool you have at your disposal to build a strong relationship. From a LinkedIn perspective, giving a recommendation to the company on their company page and an individual that you deal with on their person page, this would be a great activity to think about doing on a regular basis.

Tip 63 – Give Recommendations to Colleagues

You can recommend people that you currently work with or people that you used to work with. We talked earlier about the value of connecting with old dormant contacts, giving them a recommendation is a sure way to get them to agree to meet with you for a coffee or lunch or over Skype (depending on your location), to have a catch up. If you are a business owner then recognising an employee through a public LinkedIn recommendation is a great way to gain more engagement from that staff member, motivating them to do more, achieve more and get more results for your business.

Tip 64 – Give Recommendations to People who Refer You

You probably already have a great deal of your incoming new business from word of mouth introductions, people who refer you on a regular basis, whether that be friends and family or your existing clients spreading the word about what you offer. Just think about how much business has come in to your company from a word or mouth situation in the last 12 months alone. What have you done to thank the person who gave you a referral? Well one of many options you have is to give them a recommendation on LinkedIn.

Imagine how that person would feel if you out of the blue wrote a fantastic LinkedIn recommendation for them, as a way to thank them for the referred business they have given you. The only impact that this can have is a positive one, now they have been rewarded for an act of positivity, they are more likely to repeat that behaviour and refer you again because you thanked them through a recommendation.

Tip 65 - Get Recommendations from people who Know, Like and Trust You

I have been asked so many times to give a recommendation on LinkedIn to someone I either barely know or don't know at all. It usually comes in a spam type email where I can see it's been sent to lots of people in the hope that someone will actually take 5 minutes to do it. Essentially you should only be asking the connections you have on LinkedIn for a recommendation if you have a real business or personal relationship with them already built up. They have to know you, like you and trust you before they would even consider giving you a recommendation, so don't approach all of the LinkedIn connections you have (which believe us some people do!), be strategic, pick people that you know will say yes.

Tip 66 – Get some High Profile Recommendations

People don't just read what the recommendation says, they also look at who is giving the recommendation. Does it look better to have a bunch of recommendations from other small local business owners, or would it be better to have recommendations from a well-known brand? If you do business with a big and well known client, then try to get a personal recommendation on LinkedIn from the person you were dealing with. Large corporates very rarely provide testimonials or case studies, but they will allow their staff to give LinkedIn recommendations.

Tip 67 – Use Your Recommendations on your Website

When you receive a LinkedIn recommendation, make sure that you copy and paste it onto the testimonials page on your website. This is a great way to boost the social proof on your website that you are fantastic at what you do, and is a great way to promote the person who gave you the testimonial. If you don't already have a Testimonials section on your site, then make sure that you create one for all those new recommendations you will be receiving after reading this book!

Tip 68 – Share Your Recommendations on other Social Media Networks

Once you get a LinkedIn recommendation, talk about it and share it with your other social media networks. Put a link to it on your Facebook page, use a quote from it on Twitter, copy it onto a Google+ post, just let people know outside of LinkedIn that people are recommending you on LinkedIn. Sharing success and great things people are saying about you outside of the LinkedIn community shows that you are someone that others should be turning to for your product or service.

Tip 69 – Generate Recommendations for each Strand of 'You'

So you are on LinkedIn primarily as a business tool, however you will have many facets to your work and personal life. For example you may be involved in charity or voluntary work, you may be involved in an industry standards federation or organisation, you may do work at the local school, attend Rotary or Lions. It is important that people see you through LinkedIn as someone that has outside interests and each strand of you as a person could be recommended.

So you should try to build up recommendations for all of the different hats that you wear. It shows your character and personality and shows you in a different light. It can also be a way to open up common ground and build relationships with people that may not have considered you from a business perspective before but once they see you doing other work outside of your core business it can shed a different light on a person, especially if there are super recommendations that go with it.

Tip 70 – Ensure that you have at least 10 Recommendations Showing

As an absolute minimum we suggest that you have at least 10 recommendations for your current business or role in order to give you enough of a credibility factor to look great to someone new reading your profile. This is a good goal to set for yourself if you are not already at 10 recommendations. Start by giving first, you will immediately get some back.

LinkedIn suggests that you recommend the person back when you receive one. Focus on giving and you will find that naturally your number of recommendations goes up. If you do have people in your network that you could start with to ask them, then great but only really ask people who have either already emailed you with great feedback on what you did for them or people who have written a testimonial that you already use on literature or on your website and ask it they would mind creating one for you on LinkedIn.

10 Tips for LinkedIn Groups

LinkedIn = Member of 50 Groups, Active in at least 5

LinkedOut = Inactive member of a few LinkedIn Groups

Tip 71 - Choose Your Groups to Join

You can be a member of only 50 groups at one time. Choose wisely as you will have to leave one of your groups to join another group. You can only own/manage a maximum of 10 groups. There are 2 types of groups:

- Open – Your application to join is automatic, with no vetting by a Group Manager

- Closed – you need to request to join the group and then be approved by the Group Manager

We would recommend that you are member of different types of groups. Some from your own industry/profession, some from your target market and possibly some for a general interest that you have. The main value of groups comes in being able to connect and network with your target market.

Use the LinkedIn Groups Directory to find one of 1.5million+ specialist groups on LinkedIn.

Tip 72 – Create Your Own Group

What we really like about the Groups function is the possibility to set up your own groups if there is one that doesn't suit your needs. This is a potentially huge reputation building opportunity for your

LinkedIn profile. When you create a group, find a niche that no-one else is fulfilling and dedicate time to set it up well, manage it and use this opportunity to flood your LinkedIn profile with new contacts, new prospects and huge visibility for you and your brand.

Here are a few types of groups that are currently on LinkedIn:

- Corporate

- College / Event alumni

- Non-Profit

- Trade organizations

- Conferences

- Industry-specific

When you create your group, choose from the above list, give it a catchy and relevant name and then start promoting the group. Once your group has a presence on LinkedIn, you'll be able to search and contact fellow group members, as Group Manager you are able to communicate with the whole group not just through LinkedIn, but a group message will also be emailed out to every group member.

In 2012, Sam created a group for European Sales Agents, there was no group filling this need on LinkedIn and today the group has over 2000 members, all of whom can be contacted by Sam either individually or as a group email. It is the number one group on LinkedIn for Sales Agents, Distributors and companies looking for expansion into Europe. This has helped to profile Sam and her business and she can freely communicate with all of the members as the Group Manager. It is a great way to grow your network.

Note: Having a group Logo makes the group look more professional and it appears on the LinkedIn member's profile.

Only group owners or managers can add or edit group logos. LinkedIn doesn't allow excessive changes to a group's identity because it affects member confidence in your group and in the LinkedIn Groups product. You can only make a total of 5 group identity changes, including any group name and logo updates.

Tip 73 – How to Act in a LinkedIn Group

Whether you join an industry/profession specific group, your target market group or set up your own group, the No 1 rule is that you contribute positively. Never ever hard sell or spam the members. This will damage your reputation which is hard to build and easy to knock. Always focus on helping others, sharing useful and relevant content and engaging other group members with your knowledge, information and expertise.

Tip 74 – Set your Groups to Weekly Digest

When you join a group, you can change the settings of the group to adjust how frequently you hear from that group. You can to this by going to the tab which readse 'More…' and then choose 'Your Settings', in here there is a choice of frequency for this group. Unfortunately you cannot choose this universally across all Groups. You have to set the frequency of each Group individually.

Tip 75 – Use Groups for Industry Research

Region or Location specific industry groups are a great way of finding out what "the next big thing" in your industry/profession may be. Some regions are months/years ahead of others and this way you can keep up to date as to what may be coming down the line. You can search the 'Groups Directory' by location so refine your search results and look at what other markets and countries are doing.

Tip 76 – Keep Your Group Page Active & Fresh

Similar to your profile or company page, if you are a manager please keep your group page "fresh" with content. There is no excuse for an inactive page. You are guilty by association. Post an update relevant to the group. You can attach a link and share it on your Twitter account all at the one time if you so wish.

Tip 77 – Look out for LION's

The definition of "L.I.O.N." is a "LinkedIn Open Networker", this term is This is a designation used by several user-created groups and individual LinkedIn members to indicate a high level of interconnectivity to other LinkedIn members. This term is not endorsed by LinkedIn.

As a reminder, only join groups you want your name associated with. If you need additional information regarding any group's purpose and/or philosophy, contact the identified group owner in the Groups Directory or review the information about the Group before joining.

Tip 78 – Make it Easy for Group Members to Contact You

Communicating with a fellow group member is easy. You can send a message to a group member without being connected as long as they have this setting in place. Make sure you have the box checked that states "Allow member of this group to send me messages via LinkedIn." This needs to be selected for each group.

Tip 79 – Become Visible by being Helpful and Knowledgable

When you contribute to a Group, LinkedIn will always highlight the top influencers in the group. The more you help others in the group, the higher chance that you will be shown in the featured area of the group. If you post relevant articles, if you answer people's questions of even post new discussions then you will be demonstrating to the Group that you know what you are talking about. You will become more visible and more credible if this is done well.

You could not possibly do this in every single group you are a member of so be strategic and pick the groups where your target market is most prevalent and use this opportunity to attract more views to your profile. Stay small and use this in only a few select Groups and you will find success.

Tip 80 – Leave Groups That Are Not 'Doing It' For You

Sometimes Groups you are in can be too small, too local, too big or too annoying with commercial focus and not a networking focus. If you find yourself in a Group that is not for you, then leave it and replace it with another one.

It is quite difficult to find the small link that allows you to leave a Group. Simply visit the Group you want to leave, then go to the tab that states 'More…' then click on 'Group Settings'. Once you are in the group settings, scroll to the bottom, and find the button that says 'Leave Group'. Once you leave a Group, replace it with another one.

There are over 1.5million niche groups on LinkedIn, use the Groups Directory to find and refine your search to one that meets your needs.

10 Tips to Become the 'Go To' Expert in Your Niche

LinkedIn = You Don't Have to Look For Clients, they Come to You

LinkedOut = You are Constantly Looking for New Business

If you work LinkedIn well, you will find that you attract people to your profile almost like a spider in a web. This section is all about positioning yourself as an industry expert, the person people go to when they need a specific skill, product or service. The more you can climb the niche ladder the better, the ladder contains 4 descriptions, and it's about moving yourself from being in with the crowd to the top of the tree, once you get there you can charge more for what you do and compete with less people.

Generalists

Many people who do what you do are generalists, along with about 70% of the market, these people cut prices to compete, and they are fighting to win new clients claiming to be everything to everyone. These people earn the least amount of business and will always be struggling financially because they have no defined niche or expertise. This may be you, or not, either way the quicker you move out the generalist space the better.

You find generalists in every sector, from Recruitment to Accountancy to Printing to Marketing. Think about who you compete with and also analyse your own business are you one of hundreds of generalists? If so you will find it harder to stand out on LinkedIn.

Specialists

The next bracket up is what are known as 'Specialists', these are people who have chosen to specialise in a particular area and consists of about 25% of the market. For example, there is a Financial Advisor that both of us know, who specialises in helping families with children who have special needs. He is the only person in Ireland who specialises in this challenging field and knows how best to help families who need it, he is able to get grants, apply for funding and ensure that the children have a brighter financial future by working with the parents. As a result he has a name in the market, is referred on a regular basis and is becoming a go-to expert locally on this subject.

By having a LinkedIn profile that reflects your speciality you are going to come up first in specific searches and have significant credibility against your competition, people who specialise can gain significant market share in their space. What could you do to specialise more?

Authority or Expert

When you become an authority on a particular subject then you can start to really ramp up your visibility and credibility, there are only a small percentage (3-4%) of people in your field who elevate themselves to this level. There is no co-incidence that the word 'authority' has the word 'Author' in it! If you want to become an authority or be seen as an expert in your field, then the best activity you could work on is writing a book.

You will see that your credibility skyrockets, you will attract people to your profile on LinkedIn and other social media sites, and you will be booked more for both consultancy work and speaking opportunities if you are considered an Expert or an Authority in your chosen line of work.

Celebrity

When we use the word celebrity, it does not mean Hollywood film star or pop sensation, it means that you are the number 1 go-to person globally for what you do. Take Life Coaching and NLP, Tony Robbins would be considered the 'celebrity' in this niche, take the world of networking, Dr. Ivan Misner, founder of BNI (Business Network International) would be considered the 'celebrity' in this niche. Both of these people have written multiple best-selling books and are world famous.

Tony Robbins packs out conferences and seminars with tens of thousands of people paying hundreds of thousands of dollars to see him, he charges infinite amounts for appearances at corporate events, personal consultations and more. Why? Because the world sees this person as the 'go-to' person in their field, less than 1% of people who do what you do ever get to this level of status. If you really want to know how to become a Key Person of Influence, we recommend the book 'KPI' by Daniel Priestly. This is all about finding and dominating in a particular niche.

So how does this all relate to LinkedIn? The next 10 tips are all going to focus on how you can start to position yourself on LinkedIn as someone who knows what they are talking about in your chosen field of expertise.

Tip 81 – Frequently Share Content via LinkedIn That Reflects Your Knowledge

Share articles, blogs, reports, presentations and videos that relate to your industry and be the first to post about them. This will help to position you as someone who has their finger on the pulse and is in the know about your field of expertise. There should be about one article per day going up to show that you know what you are talking about.

Tip 82 – Use Automation Tools - Twitterfeed

If you cannot be on LinkedIn every day but you want to guarantee that there is great content feeding your LinkedIn profile (and of course other online networks), then using a free automation tool such as Twitterfeed will help you to look like you are always using LinkedIn and feeding great information to your network.

You use Twitterfeed by finding a blog or article stream that you like, are happy with and constantly puts out great content you would be happy to share. If you are in Business Coaching you might choose HBR (Harvard Business Review), if you are in Online Marketing you might choose Hubspot etc.

Then you follow the 3 simple steps on Twitterfeed once your account is set up and choose the frequency of posts plus which online sites you want to feed the latest articles out to, and you are done. This way you can always share information first and show your LinkedIn contacts that you are on top of your industry, helping you to position yourself as someone who is in the know all the time.

You can learn more about Twitterfeed here: http://twitterfeed.com

Tip 83 – Start a Blog or get someone to Blog for you

If you don't find the time or don't have the inclination to write a book, then blogging can be one of the best ways to position yourself as an expert. In relation to LinkedIn you can use your status updates to get your blog into Groups, into your status updates and shared with your wider networks. Blogging not only helps position you as an expert in your field, it also helps your website to appear in search rankings on Google and helps to build a list which you can then market your product or service to.

Always remember that blogging is about sharing great content for free, and in no way should it be used for selling. Great blogs get shared, they increase your visibility and of course your credibility. You will generate new leads and prospects from blogging and your LinkedIn profile can be used to share your blog. You can add a link to your profile on LinkedIn both in the contact section of your Personal Profile, a link on your Company Page and also a link added to your Personal Summary.

If you don't have the time to write articles then use sites such as http://Fiverr.com to outsource this to people happy to write great content for websites for as little as $5.00.

Tip 84 – Use Relevant Keywords for your Niche on Your Profile

We already talked about the importance of keywords for your professional headline, always ensure that the main niche keywords run throughout your LinkedIn profile, summary, current job(s) and company page. If your niche is very specific, not too many people are going to pop up in LinkedIn searches when they go looking for someone that does what you do. This will help you to position yourself as an expert in your niche.

Tip 85 – Give away Freebies via LinkedIn

Free is a great way to get people interested in your niche, giving away free reports, free content, free resources and tools is a fantastic way to show people that you know what you are doing in your space. As an example, in the low cost online recruitment business owned and managed by Sam Rathling, companies can gain access to a free recruitment cost analysis tool. This positions Recruitment Magic as a 'go to' expert when it comes to analysing and reducing the recruitment cost for companies.

You'll see in the free chapter which is being given away at the end of this book that there are 3 free business templates to use which help business owners to become better givers, and by doing so they grow their business. This positions Sam (known as 'The Givingpreneur') as a person who knows all about giving to grow a business. What could you give away in your business? A great place to give away freebies is through your LinkedIn profile. If you visit Sam's Linked In profile and ask her to connect with you. You will see that she gives away a free chapter of the book (the same one you will gain access to at the end of this book) and again it helps to position Sam as an expert or authority in a niche area.

Connect with Sam on LinkedIn here:
http://ie.linkedin.com/in/samrathling

Tip 86 – Become a Speaker & Profile Yourself as a Speaker on LinkedIn

Even if you are new to public speaking, you can use your LinkedIn profile to position yourself as a Speaker on your subject. Even if you have only done a few local events, and even if they were not paid you can really start to use your LinkedIn presence to get invited to speak at more events. You can offer yourself as a speaker through organisations, networks, professional bodies and more. Your LinkedIn profile could get you booked for many speaking engagements especially if you choose a niche that few people occupy.

If you are going to dominate in your chosen field of expertise then you should learn the skills you need to present in front of an audience, you can highlight your speaking topics and experience on your LinkedIn profile. This tip won't be for everyone, but if you work LinkedIn well and focus on this aspect of your niche then you will find that you get booked more and more, and you can start charging more for fees to speak. We regularly get booked to speak at conferences and events as experts in LinkedIn, very few people speak well on this subject and both of us are regularly booked through our online networks to speak and consult with companies who are looking to generate more business from LinkedIn.

Tip 87 – Respond to Discussions in Groups

You can use the Groups to your advantage by looking out for discussions started by other members in the group where people are looking for help on a subject which you know a great deal about. So if you are into reducing costs for companies, you could join the group 'Cost Reduction Strategies' on LinkedIn and keep a look out for posts where people are asking for help in reducing a specific aspect of their business. Always remember to respond with useful advice, in a non-sales way to help the other person solve their issue.

Active members of groups are profiled by LinkedIn and other members of the group will see you regularly contributing to help others. The groups function can be a great way to position yourself as an expert in your field and will help you to generate new clients.

Tip 88 – Keep an eye on your Profile Views

What we would like you to do now after reading this book is to check your current number of times your profile has been viewed in the last 'X' number of days. It will be different for every reader as some of you will be more active on LinkedIn than others. Write down that number, this is now going to be referred to as your 'Visibility Factor'.

Our goal as Authors is to ensure that your profile views is increasing all the time and that you are attracting people to your profile through all of the techniques we have shared here. The great news is that whatever your number is today, it is going to go up considerably by just taking a few small simple steps to increase your visibility.

Tip 89 – Check how often you appear in Search Results

Now look in the same place, on your home page on the right hand side you will see how many times you have appeared in search results. When you choose 'See More' then you will be taken to a page full of statistics about your LinkedIn visibility. This will tell you how well your new profile is working, based on the keywords that you have used in your profile. The more times you appear in search results the more likely that someone will connect with you, find you or do business with you. 5.7 billion searches took place on LinkedIn in 2012, our goal is to ensure that you appear in more of these search results from now onwards than when you did before you read this book.

Write down now the number of times you have appeared in search results in 'X' number of days and keep tracking it as the weeks go on. You will see a dramatic change in your search appearances.

Tip 90 – Regularly make changes to your Profile

LinkedIn likes to email its members with regular updates about what is happening in your network of contacts. So if someone changes a job title, or starts a new position in a new company or is celebrating a work anniversary, then LinkedIn will share this via an email summary. They will also share when people add new items to their profile. The key to appearing on this 'Updates' is to regularly change your profile. You might tweak your professional headline, you might slightly change your job title even if you are in the same company and role for example. Either way keep your profile up to date, and frequently change your information, as everytime you do your name appears in the Activity Feed and you will also stand a chance of being in the update email that LinkedIn sends to your contacts.

10 Tips for Extra LinkedIn Learning

LinkedIn = Always learning about LinkedIn and what it can do for you

LinkedOut = Stopping learning after you finish this book

Tip 91 – Follow Top Twitter Influencers for LinkedIn Tips and Updates

These people are great to follow for LinkedIn Tips and Updates, if you are on Twitter then simply follow these links and start following these key influencers who regularly tweet about LinkedIn:

@LinkedIn

@LinkedInToday

@LinkedInHelp

@LinkedInExpert

@LinkedInTrainer

@theLinkedInGuy

@LinkedInDiva

@Learn_LinkedIn

@LinkedInQueen

@danLinkedInman

@BurdaLinkedIn

And of course you can follow the co-Authors of this book:

Sam Rathling: @samrathling and Derek Reilly: @derekreilly

Tip 92 – Take Home Study Courses to Upskill

There are a number of home study courses available, which go into a lot more depth on LinkedIn that we have been able to cover here. This course is one we recommend and is a good basis for all of your LinkedIn needs if you are more visual and need a combination of text, audio and video:

LinkedIn Home Study Course

Tip 93 – Download best-selling book "How to Really Use LinkedIn" for free

We are big fans of this book and if you are very new to LinkedIn it really is a step-by-step guide, and goes into a lot more detail than this book with images and pictures. In true 'Givers Gain' style, the author is giving away 1 million copies for free. We said at the start that this book was full of simple tips that you could use a checklist to start doing more in LinkedIn. We recommend this book to all of our clients who want to increase their knowledge even more:

http://www.how-to-really-use-linkedin.com/

Tip 94 – Read 17 of the Best LinkedIn Articles we could find

This is a blog written by Sam Rathling which was to coincide with LinkedIn's achievement of getting to 200 million members. The blog features 17 of the best LinkedIn articles available on the internet and is great extra reading in addition to this book:

http://www.samrathling.com/tips-for-linkedin/

Tip 95 – Visit the LinkedIn Help Center

If you are ever stuck on any aspect of LinkedIn and you don't have this book to hand, then you can always visit the LinkedIn Help Center. You can find this link in the top right-hand corner of your LinkedIn profile.

You can access the LinkedIn Help Center here: http://help.linkedin.com/

Tip 96 – Check out "The LinkedIn Guy" Video Coaching Series

Our good friend, Rick Itzkowich aka "The LinkedIn Guy" has a great video based coaching offer which is the one I always recommend to my clients. To learn more about Rick's online tips for LinkedIn and to become a part of a great community of LinkedIn learners, then you can learn more here. Rick also has a LinkedIn Group which you can participate in here.

http://www.rickitzkowich.com/

Tip 97 – Follow the LinkedIn Blog

You can read the official LinkedIn Blog on this link. It will always keep you up to date with the latest updates and changes happening on LinkedIn: http://blog.linkedin.com/

Tip 98 – Take a "LinkedIn or LinkedOut?" Masterclass

Derek Reilly and Sam Rathling deliver a one day version of all of the content in this book and more to Corporates, Business Owners and Sales Teams. If you want to really get more from LinkedIn and you have enjoyed the content of this book then you could benefit from a full day with one or both of the Authors. There are also webinars available. If you want to be kept up to date with when these are courses and webinars are running, then you can sign up for news updates here by opting in to our mailing list. We hate spam as much as you do so we will not bombard you with emails or sell your information to third parties, that's a promise!

Tip 99 – Get a LinkedIn Personal Coach

If you don't have the time or inclination to put into action everything we have spoken about here in this easy to read and simple to follow book, then you may benefit from having your own personal LinkedIn coach. Contact us on info@samrathling.com for details of personal LinkedIn coaching services and a list of recommended people to contact for this 1:1 customised service.

Tip 100 – Follow the Authors Blog

Sam and Derek regularly blog about LinkedIn and other topics in relation to business networking, you can follow these posts at http://samrathling.com.

7 Additional Tips to Help You Win More Clients

LinkedIn = A LinkedIn Member who wins new business from LinkedIn

LinkedOut = No new clients from LinkedIn

Tip 101 – Promote your LinkedIn Public Profile

Put a link to your LinkedIn profile on the bottom of your email signatures, and include the link to your profile on your website, blog and other social media sites. Let people know that you can be found on LinkedIn. Ask them to connect with you. Use the public profile URL we talked about in Tip 5, in the very first section of this book.

You can also use this link on your website, on your blog, your business card and other social media sites to encourage more people to connect with you on LinkedIn. You are missing an opportunity if you do not let people know how to connect with you.

Tip 102 – Combine Online Networking with Offline Networking

Networking is about finding out how you can help people and then doing it! Always focus on how you can help another connection first, remember that you first need to build credibility by relationship building, helping the other person in some way could be connecting them to someone in your network or sharing an article that will help them and is relevant to their business.

We call this "Givers Gain"® which is the philosophy of Business Network International or BNI as it is widely known as. BNI is the world's largest and most successful referral organisation with over 150,000 members worldwide in over 50 countries. Both Derek and Sam who wrote this book are passionate about BNI, both involved at Director level, helping members across Ireland and other countries to grow their business through the power of giving. If you help enough other people to get what they want, you will in return get what you want.

So if you take this concept to LinkedIn, if you help enough other people in your network it will all come back to you, this is based on the old adage of 'what goes around, comes around'. If you love online networking using sites like LinkedIn then you will also love BNI. We recommend that you find a local chapter of BNI and go along to see how it could help your business to grow. If you are new to networking or if you want to learn how to be a more effective networker then this could be a huge opportunity for your business.

Tip 103 – Never, Ever, Ever Sell!

The number one rule when it comes to online networking is to steer clear of any form of selling. Don't use LinkedIn to hunt, prospect or sell.

This is the biggest turn off for most people and yet we constantly see people bombarding their contacts with messages spamming everyone in their LinkedIn contacts with message to buy a product or click on a website, with no relationship having been built. If you want to generate more business through LinkedIn then do not use it as a sales platform.

Tip 104 – Research People You Are Going to Meet

When you have a meeting planned with a new contact, it can be a very useful exercise to go through the person's LinkedIn profile before you meet them. Look at 2 things:

- Their Information

Looking at someone's information will help you to build rapport and the relationship, especially if you find something on the LinkedIn profile that you have as a mutual or common interest. You could bring this topic up in conversation and suddenly you'll just click and the person is more likely to do business with you or want to help you.

- Their Connections

Once you know who you are going to be meeting, take a look at their LinkedIn connections. You will be able to see how many shared contacts you have as well as identify if they know someone that could be of use to you, whether that be a potential referral partner, introducer, end client or supplier. Be prepared going into your meeting and again, find a way to bring up the person or contact you are looking for.

Tip 105 – Use LinkedIn to Hold More Effective Face to Face Meetings

When you sit down with a new contact, you will want to help the other person and see how you can be of assistance to them. Quite often, one of the most powerful ways to build the relationship face to face is to offer to connect the person to someone you know. This introduction could prove to be invaluable and will come back to you in more ways than one.

So always have your LinkedIn contacts handy, ideally the LinkedIn mobile App, for your Smartphone or Tablet. Make sure that you refer to LinkedIn during every face to face meeting. Offer your connections to the other person, ask them to take a look through and if there is someone there that they would like to meet to just let you know.

This will move your credibility factor up and the person will want to help you in some way. This is where you can leverage the knowledge you have already gained about their network from looking them up before you arranged to meet. This will take your face to face meetings to a new level and will allow you to grow your business by attracting more referrals, positive word of mouth about you and your business as well as delivering some great contacts back to you.

Tip 106 – Generate leads using LinkedIn

By using the Advanced Search Tools that we have already looked at in this book, you can really start to use LinkedIn as a lead generation tool. Once you have searched for people that you would like to do business with, ask them to connect with you, then follow up with a soft non-sales driven message. You'll be surprised how willing people are to connect and hear what you have to say if you don't do it in a pushy way.

You can generate real leads and opportunities on LinkedIn, you just need to be diligent and disciplined on it. Set goals for yourself around how many people you will approach in a week, how many follow up messages you will send and you'll see instant results if you start taking action, tracking and measuring the impact of your proactive use of this amazing business platform.

Tip 107 – Give, Give and Give Some More

It is vital that you remember the VCP Process in all that you do, as well as focusing on helping others in your LinkedIn network, by giving first. As this is the last tip in the book (besides a bonus chapter taken from the book "GIVE: 16 Giving Strategies to Grow Your Business"), it feels right that the last tip is give, give and give some more. This is one of the most powerful ways to generate business opportunities. There are many ways for you to give online, and then transfer this into your face to face business networking. We will leave you with our favourite quote about giving:

"We make a living by what we get, but we make a life by what we give" **Winston Churchill**

And Finally…

So we have come to the end of the list of 107 Tips to Grow Your Business using LinkedIn, remember to visit this page to get your download of the tips as a PDF so you can check off your progress and not have to constantly refer back to the book:

http://samrathling.com/107-Tips-Checklist-For-LinkedIn

We would like to genuinely thank you for purchasing this book, which we hope you have found useful. Over time as you implement the steps, you will start to see your profile views increasing, your appearance in search results going up and your ability to engage, connect with and manage your contacts get easier.

The impact and effectiveness of your online networking will over time start to win you more clients, new opportunities and help you to grow your business. We now hope you feel more LinkedIn than LinkedOut. To Your Success!

Free Chapter from 'GIVE: 16 Giving Strategies To Grow Your Business' by Sam Rathling

Enjoy this gift from your co-Author Sam Rathling, who wrote and published "GIVE: 16 Giving Strategies To Grow Your Business" in March 2013. This book has more than twenty-five, 5-star reviews on Amazon and achieved #1 best-selling status in the Small Business category on Amazon in its first month.

You can be assured that you will pick up some great tips and tools to use in your business by reading this bonus chapter.

Chapter 3 - Giving Meetings

In the previous chapter on giving goals, we looked at setting goals for activities that primarily revolve around helping another person. In this chapter we will explore the concept of a giving meeting. In the beginning of this book I shared with you my story upon first arriving in Ireland. Do you remember Patrick, who I met first at a networking event, then arranged to meet me for a coffee? Patrick and I are still in touch and he is a very valued client in my business, he now works in international sales for ASEA, (an amazing product), and is no longer in the print industry. Do you recall that he spent 90 minutes in that meeting focusing 100% on me and what he could do to help me? That is what I now refer to as a giving meeting and this is how I approach every new connection and prospective referral partner or potential client.

This again may involve a shift in your mindset and way of thinking about the meetings that you hold from now on. Because every sales training presentation you attend and many books you read about how to get new business involve how you can get your sales message across to the other person. Often you will read or hear tips on how to communicate your features and benefits to them in a way that helps them to buy from you. Yes there is some focus on the other person, but this usually involves asking questions to understand their needs so that you can hen pitch your solutions, products or service to the person in front of you.

The giving meeting is an act of helping another person. The sole purpose of your time you spend with the other person is to understand their business, and what you can do to help them first. A real giving meeting is a 100% dedication to the other person and their business.

This chapter will give you a template to work from with a set of questions that will enable you to really give and help them. In order to help the other person you need to understand their business and open up opportunities for you to help them, refer them and create a long-lasting relationship.

The Giving Meeting Template

The following questions are to be used in a giving meeting to establish rapport, build the relationship and understand how you can help them. Once you know this information about the other person and you feel comfortable referring them to your network then it will be much easier for you to help them in some way:

Question 1 - Tell me about yourself and how you got into this business

This question allows you to relax the other person, they will feel comfortable sharing their background and history and you can learn a lot from the person by having them talk about what they did before. The advantage for you is that you get to find out what contacts the person may have based on their previous career. You are not going to use this information now, but it should be stored and recorded after the meeting. When you have helped this person first, they will want to help you back in the future. By understanding their contacts from past roles, you may secure an opportunity of an introduction further down the line.

Question 2 - What is it that you love about what you do?

This question allows the person you are trying to help to talk about their passion. You will quite often see body language change and a more animated response. Everyone loves to talk about their passions and what they love to do. This again is part of the relationship building process. If you know what they love about their work, you know that they will be most responsive when you refer them a contact or a piece of business which involves what they love to work on.

Question 3 - What are the main products and services you offer to clients?

This question is more of a fact-finding exercise. If you've not had a chance to do your homework on the company before the meeting then this is an opportunity to learn about the products and services on offer.

Question 4 - After you have delivered your products /services what results does the client see?

This is really asking the question what value do you add. This should be where you find out the benefits of working with the company you are trying to help. Quite often the products and services are the main focus of a meeting like this, but if you truly want to help the person then you need to know how they deliver results for their clients. Do they save client's money? Do they reduce stress? Do they give peace of mind? It is really finding out what the clients they work for are left with after they have delivered their service or products. What do they feel, think, do or have AFTER the company has delivered their work.

Question 5 - What makes you totally unique and different from your competition?

This is all about USP's (Unique Selling Points). The person you are meeting needs to clearly communicate their points of difference if you are going to be able to help them. The issue is that most small businesses cannot really identify their absolute unique selling points. They use descriptions like 'we give really personal service', however that really is not a unique selling point. It may be true, but all of their competition is out there saying that too.

Question 6 - What professions or categories of business are you looking to talk to?

This question is all about identifying potential strategic alliances or referral partners for the person you are trying to help. You could introduce them to an end customer who spends with them once, or you could introduce them to a connection who could pass them multiple clients. An example of this would be a video production company. You could introduce them to an SME who wants to make a video for their website, or even better would be to introduce them to a marketing agency who outsource all of their video production work. Which is the more valuable contact? The second one of course because of the potential number of clients that it could bring. The more you help them with strategic alliances and referral partners, the more will come back to you.

Question 7 - What are the names of the top 20 companies you would love to do business with?

This is a question that many small business owners cannot answer off the top of their head. Quite often the target market for a company starts with 'Anyone who...' or 'Any company that...'. If you can get a list of the dream clients that the person in front of you is looking to do business with than you can be much more specific in your quest to help them. Go back to the giving meeting I had with Patrick, he asked me this question but I was prepared and had already created a top 100 prospect client list from business directories and LinkedIn.

I was able to name companies that I wanted to work with and he was able to facilitate an introduction for me to someone on the list. If the person you are meeting is not prepared, ask them to list for you the last 10 customers they did business with. This will give you a chance to see the types of companies that they help.

In addition the assumption would be that if they have already done business with one haulage/logistics company that they would like to be introduced to more haulage and logistics companies. Then you can start to help them be more specific.

Question 8 - What questions can I ask a potential client to help open up the opportunity for you?

You could be standing in the middle of a referral opportunity for the person in front of you, but unless you know what to say in the situation you could blow it. This question is really to get an idea of what the person you are trying to help would say if they met someone looking to buy their product or service. By having 2 or 3 key questions to qualify the opportunity you will make it much easier to pass on the person's details to a potential client. It also means that the referral is more likely to happen and be the kind of opportunity that they are looking for because you have been armed with the right questions to ask. I have an electrician in my network who I use personally and refer to other people. He helps companies to reduce their electricity bill through an energy audit. Every time I see spotlights in a venue, office, or house I simply ask "Do you know how much those are costing you?". This starts a conversation and allows me to move into a potential referral situation where I can help him with a new client.

Question 9 - How can I introduce you? What do you want me to say on your behalf?

If you can get a one liner, easy to remember from the person you are helping it will be so much easier to create an opportunity for them. For the electrician I simply say "I know a great electrician who can save you up to 80% on your electricity bill through a free energy audit. I highly recommend him and he's saved me a fortune!". When you are in your giving meeting, try to identify what to say on behalf of the person you are helping to make it easy to refer them. This is especially important if they work in the type of business where everyone already has a supplier such as an

Accountant or a Printer. It has to be more compelling than just "I know a great [insert profession] can I get him to give you a call?"

Question 10 - Can you tell me a story about how you recently helped a client?

If you are stuck on question 9, or if the person you are meeting is stuck then this may help. Facts tell and stories sell, so this is where you can get the person to share success stories and how they help their clients. From this you may also find a good one liner introduction. It is far easier to remember a compelling story than a list of features and benefits, and combine this with emotion and you will have an easy way to help the person, simply by relaying the great story about how they help their clients.

Question 11 - What am I going to hear or see in my everyday settings that could indicate an opportunity for you?

This last question is really to help you determine triggers that you may see or hear when you are out and about that will make you think of this persons business. If you go back to the electrician, he has trained me to look out for spotlights whenever I am in people's homes or in a commercial premises such as a hotel or an office. He knows how much he can save a venue or household. So every time I see spotlights I think of the electrician. Armed with my one question "Do you know how much those are costing you?", combined with my how to introduce you ""I know a great electrician who can save you up to 80% on your electricity bill through a free energy audit. I highly recommend him and he's saved me a fortune!"

Question 12 - Where do you network?

This is a great question to ask a new person in your network, they may be attending events that you were not aware of and they may be happy to take you along and introduce you to potential new contacts. Share each others interests and networks outside of the main business and you never know what you might uncover. Either way it will really help you to form a strong relationship, find common ground and lead to future opportunities.

So you get to the end of the giving meeting, and now you have lots of information gathered from the other person. The final thing to do is to close the meeting by summarising back to the person what information you have taken down. You could also then arrange a follow up meeting date where you agree to meet up for a second time to go through the actions arising from this first meeting.

It is likely that during the 12 questions you determined a number of ways to help the other person. Now it's all about follow up. The most important thing is that if you agreed to take action or do something for them that you actually do it. Having this follow up meeting brings some accountability in and will ensure that you DWYSYAGTD! (Do What You Say You Are Going To Do!).

The Giving Meeting Template Download

To make things easy for you and to help you with your Giving Meetings, I have created a template for you to download. Simply visit this link and you can download a free PDF template for you to use in your giving meetings.

http://samrathling.com/giving-meeting-template

One suggestion I have for you to make your giving activity produce results, is that you create a document for your own business using this template of questions too. Imagine at the end of a giving meeting the person you are helping asks how they can help you back, or later in the relationship they are looking to help you in some way. The best thing to do is be prepared for this as it will happen.

The 121 Toolkit Template Download

My recommendation is to send back your version of these questions in a document so that they have a complete overview of your business and how they can help you. Imagine if every time you met someone new in your network, that they took away with them the list of answers to these 12 questions for your business.

Once again, I am going to make this real easy for you (a theme running throughout this book!). You can download an editable word document for you to complete for your own business, I call this a 121 Toolkit. It's something you can use in both giving meetings and in other meetings that involve you presenting your business to a potential referral partner, strategic alliance, supplier or client.

I have been using this myself for years, and more recently have been giving this to clients and other people in my network and to date it has produced some staggering results. One of the best stories I know about this document involves a lady based in Manchester in the UK. She had been struggling to get new clients into her alternative healing business. People in her network just didn't 'get' her business and didn't know how to refer her.

After hearing about this 121 Toolkit, she created this document for her business in preparation for a 10 minute presentation she was giving the following week to her networking group. At the end of the presentation she gave a copy of this 121 Toolkit to the group to take away with them. Bear in mind, she had not received a single referral in 7 months from this group of people. The week after giving the 121 Toolkit in hard copy to her networking group which detailed more specifically what she was looking for, she was given 19 referrals!! Yes, she went from zero referrals in 7 months, to 19 in just one week! Now if that story doesn't motivate you to get one of these for your business then you may as well stop reading now, because there is more great stuff to come in the other chapters too.

You can download your 121 Toolkit template here:

http://samrathling.com/121-toolkit-template

So now you know how to make your giving meetings work for you, and of course the person you are looking to help with their business. In addition you have a great tool to use for your own business to really focus the people in your network on how they can help you back. It can take some time to put together a great 121 Toolkit but it is well worth the effort for the results it will deliver back to your business.

Next we are going to spend some time on Giving Gratitude, as I am sure when you start giving help to others you will start to hear the words 'Thank You' a lot more, and you will also need some great ideas on how to say 'Thank You' to others when the new opportunities and clients start rolling in to your business.

Actions & Ideas on Giving Meetings

1. Think about 3 people you have recently met that you could hold a giving meeting with and write down their name.

2. Visit the link and download the giving meeting template, start using this with all new connections you meet.

3. Create your own version of a 121 Toolkit so that you have something to give a person when they ask how they can help you back.

To get your paperback copy of the whole book "GIVE: 16 Giving Strategies To Grow Your Business click here:

Amazon.co.uk Customers:
http://amzn.to/10GcF95

Amazon.com Customers:
http://amzn.to/10Xcaq5

If you prefer the digital version then use these links to get the full digital version:

Amazon.co.uk Customers: http://amzn.to/YkaE7d
Amazon.com Customers: http://amzn.to/167XVnC

If you don't have a Kindle you can use this link to download the free Kindle reading App: http://amzn.to/XTHawP

About The Authors – Sam Rathling

Sam Rathling is originally from the UK, and is now based in Cork, Ireland, she is married to Andoly, and together they have 3 children, Oscar, Maya and Liliana. Life is hectic, fun and spent mostly helping other people to achieve results through speaking, training and writing.

Sam is an Entrepreneur in the recruitment industry, with a focus on providing low cost recruitment solutions to give SME's a low cost alternative to the traditional recruitment agency via her business, RecruitmentMagic.com.

Sam is considered an expert in online and offline networking, having written best-selling book 'GIVE: 16 Giving Strategies To Grow Your Business' and contributed to another best-selling book 'Building the Ultimate Network', she now speaks across the world sharing her networking success story, inspiring people to take action through giving and helping others.

Her expertise on LinkedIn, sees her travel the world delivering a very popular LinkedIn Masterclass which accompanies this book 'LinkedIn or LinkedOut'. Sam's practical courses show you how to achieve massive results with LinkedIn which is suitable for SME's and corporate sales teams. Sam delivers LinkedIn training both face to face and online, her online training series is due for release in late 2013.

Sam has successfully achieved what many business owners hope to do, which is to work less hours and spend more time with her family. She has successfully gone from a 70 hour week, to a 20 hour week, earning more money as a result.

Sam is currently writing more books, the next is **"How Does She Do It All? The Definitive Guide for Mumpreneurs, for Mums who want to work less, earn more and spend more time with their kids"**. All of Sam's non-fiction books help you to grow your business through effective online and offline networking, relationship building and giving. If you wish to know when the next book is coming out and to hear all of the latest news from Sam, you can stay in touch by doing some or all of the following:

Follow Sam on Twitter: @samrathling

Connect with Sam on LinkedIn: http://ie.linkedin.com/in/samrathling

Subscribe to SamRathling.com: http://samrathling.com

Amazon Author Central Page:

http://www.amazon.com/Sam-Rathling/e/B00BU93ZD4

Learn more about Sam's seminars, workshops, business mentoring, products and more at http://ELITEforbusiness.com

About The Authors – Derek Reilly

Derek Reilly is based in the West of Ireland. He lives in a little remote town that looks out over the Atlantic Ocean.

He is surrounded by his friends and family where he is the eldest of 5 boys. He is a very proud uncle to Paige and godfather to Kate.

Derek is known as the "LinkedIn Leprechaun" able to find the pot of gold at the end of the LinkedIn rainbow. The funny thing is, at 6'2" tall, he is the tallest leprechaun you will ever meet!

If more success and personal development is what you're seeking, then Derek can help you get from where you are to where you want to be.

He has personally trained hundreds of businesses using his friendly and approachable style while maximising the potential from the workshop material. As a natural born trainer, Derek gets a real buzz from seeing the "light bulb" moment turning on in the attendee heads.

Derek is a fully qualified Trainer with:

- Mayo Fire and Rescue Service (where he has being a fireman and now officer since 2001).

- JCI or Junior Chamber International (where he is the Deputy National President of JCI Ireland 2013).

- BNI (Business Network International) in Ireland South and West. He is an Area Director Consultant responsible for launching, supporting and training Business Networking groups. He has been with BNI since 2007.

Gaining acclaim for his knowledge in the art of Business Networking and how to use LinkedIn, Derek now speaks on the topic both nationally and internationally as well as other topics including Klout.

Follow Derek on Twitter: @derekreilly

Connect with Derek on LinkedIn:
http://ie.linkedin.com/in/derekreilly/

Before You Go…

It's now the end of this book, all about how to get more business from LinkedIn. We hope you genuinely learnt something new and found these tips useful. If you liked it and you think other small business owners would benefit from this knowledge then we would really appreciate a review of this book on Amazon.

Thank you in advance for doing this for us, it really means more to us than you realise.

Printed in Great Britain
by Amazon